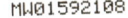

MY

TRAVEL

JOURNAL

MIRABELL PUBLISHING

A NOTE FOR PARENTS

Hi There!

Thank you for purchasing "My Travel Journal" for your child!

Our hope and aim for this travel journal, is to be able to capture and preserve special childhood memories, helping your child to write as much as they can about their holiday experiences as they develop their writing skills.

We specifically designed this travel journal for children between the ages of 5 to 9 years. This is to introduce them to the art of journaling with easy thought out questions that require brief simple answers. When all filled out, it should give a compact yet informative summary of all their holiday experiences!

When your child is all grown up, we want you to be able to look back at this journal and have a good laugh with your child. From experience, we know without a journal these little moments of joy are almost certain to be forgotten twenty years from now.

We hope you and your child enjoy using this travel journal in order to create lasting memories for generations to come.

…and remember, have fun!

Mirabell Publishing

ALL ABOUT
ME

Paste your passport photograph here!

NAME

ADDRESS

DATE OF BIRTH

AGE   **HEIGHT**

EYE COLOUR

MOBILE NUMBER

EMAIL

SIGNATURE

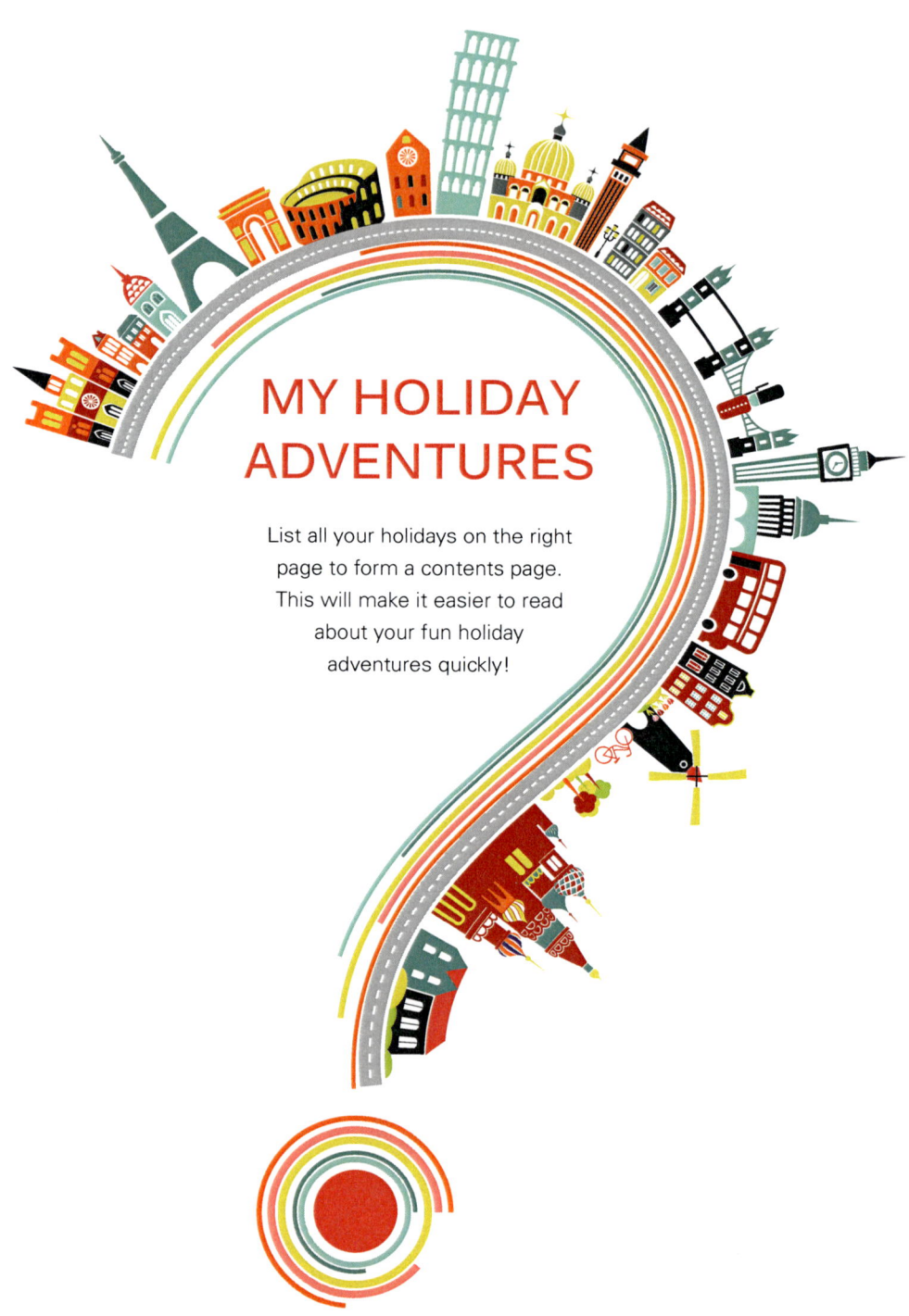

MY HOLIDAY ADVENTURES

List all your holidays on the right
page to form a contents page.
This will make it easier to read
about your fun holiday
adventures quickly!

1

MY TRIP TO

WRITE, DRAW OR PASTE PHOTOGRAPHS ABOUT YOUR
ADVENTURES ON YOUR TRIP...

MY TRAVEL BUDDIES

NAME	
RELATIONSHIP TO YOU	
TELEPHONE NUMBER	

NAME	
RELATIONSHIP TO YOU	
TELEPHONE NUMBER	

NAME	
RELATIONSHIP TO YOU	
TELEPHONE NUMBER	

NAME	
RELATIONSHIP TO YOU	
TELEPHONE NUMBER	

NAME	
RELATIONSHIP TO YOU	
TELEPHONE NUMBER	

DON'T FORGET TO...

- Turn off your computer or ask your parents to do so
- Pack your travel guide books
- Take some travel stickers, pencils, a pack of colourful pens, glue sticks and adhesive tape for your travel journal.
- Take your favourite games to play on the trip and books to read

BEFORE THE TRIP

Where are you going?	
Is this your first visit?	
What do you know about the place?	Are you travelling by road, air, train or by sea?
How are you going to get there?	Does the country have a language different to yours?
Are you going to a different country?	
What do you think the place will be like?	
What are you looking forward to the most?	
What places would you visit during the trip?	For example theme parks, museums, zoo

LEAVING HOME

What is the weather like today?	
I travelled from...	to...
How far is the trip?	
How long will it take you to get there?	

Stick a map of where you are going.

Trace a line from where you live to where you are going

Interesting things I saw on the trip	

WHERE WE'RE STAYING

Draw a picture showing where you are staying during your vacation

Things I like about where we are staying	
Interesting things I saw	
I learned some interesting things about	
My favourite meal was	
I enjoyed playing with	
I did not enjoy doing	

GOING BACK HOME

I enjoyed my vacation because...

Did you make new friends?

Would you want to go back there?

Did you bring home any souvenirs?

The thing that surprised me most was...

MY NEW FRIENDS

NAME	
EMAIL	
TELEPHONE NUMBER	

NAME	
EMAIL	
TELEPHONE NUMBER	

NAME	
EMAIL	
TELEPHONE NUMBER	

NAME	
EMAIL	
TELEPHONE NUMBER	

NAME	
EMAIL	
TELEPHONE NUMBER	

2

MY TRIP TO

WRITE, DRAW OR PASTE PHOTOGRAPHS ABOUT YOUR
ADVENTURES ON YOUR TRIP...

MY TRAVEL BUDDIES

NAME	
RELATIONSHIP TO YOU	
TELEPHONE NUMBER	

NAME	
RELATIONSHIP TO YOU	
TELEPHONE NUMBER	

NAME	
RELATIONSHIP TO YOU	
TELEPHONE NUMBER	

NAME	
RELATIONSHIP TO YOU	
TELEPHONE NUMBER	

NAME	
RELATIONSHIP TO YOU	
TELEPHONE NUMBER	

DON'T FORGET TO...

- Turn off your computer or ask your parents to do so
- Pack your travel guide books
- Take some travel stickers, pencils, a pack of colourful pens, glue sticks and adhesive tape for your travel journal.
- Take your favourite games to play on the trip and books to read

BEFORE THE TRIP

Where are you going?	
Is this your first visit?	
What do you know about the place?	Are you travelling by road, air, train or by sea?
How are you going to get there?	Does the country have a language different to yours?
Are you going to a different country?	
What do you think the place will be like?	
What are you looking forward to the most?	
What places would you visit during the trip?	For example theme parks, museums, zoo

LEAVING HOME

What is the weather like today?	

I travelled from...		to...

How far is the trip?	

How long will it take you to get there?	

Stick a map of where you are going.

Trace a line from where you live to where you are going

Interesting things I saw on the trip	

WHERE WE'RE STAYING

Draw a picture showing where you are staying during your vacation

Things I like about where we are staying	
Interesting things I saw	
I learned some interesting things about	
My favourite meal was	
I enjoyed playing with	
I did not enjoy doing	

GOING BACK HOME

I enjoyed my vacation because...

Did you make new friends?

Would you want to go back there?

Did you bring home any souvenirs?

The thing that surprised me most was...

MY NEW FRIENDS

NAME	
EMAIL	
TELEPHONE NUMBER	

NAME	
EMAIL	
TELEPHONE NUMBER	

NAME	
EMAIL	
TELEPHONE NUMBER	

NAME	
EMAIL	
TELEPHONE NUMBER	

NAME	
EMAIL	
TELEPHONE NUMBER	

3

MY TRIP TO

WRITE, DRAW OR PASTE PHOTOGRAPHS ABOUT YOUR
ADVENTURES ON YOUR TRIP...

MY TRAVEL BUDDIES

NAME	
RELATIONSHIP TO YOU	
TELEPHONE NUMBER	

NAME	
RELATIONSHIP TO YOU	
TELEPHONE NUMBER	

NAME	
RELATIONSHIP TO YOU	
TELEPHONE NUMBER	

NAME	
RELATIONSHIP TO YOU	
TELEPHONE NUMBER	

NAME	
RELATIONSHIP TO YOU	
TELEPHONE NUMBER	

DON'T FORGET TO...

- Turn off your computer or ask your parents to do so
- Pack your travel guide books
- Take some travel stickers, pencils, a pack of colourful pens, glue sticks and adhesive tape for your travel journal.
- Take your favourite games to play on the trip and books to read

BEFORE THE TRIP

Where are you going?	
Is this your first visit?	
What do you know about the place?	Are you travelling by road, air, train or by sea?
How are you going to get there?	Does the country have a language different to yours?
Are you going to a different country?	
What do you think the place will be like?	
What are you looking forward to the most?	
What places would you visit during the trip?	For example theme parks, museums, zoo

LEAVING HOME

What is the weather like today?	

I travelled from...	to...

How far is the trip?	

How long will it take you to get there?	

Stick a map of where you are going.

Trace a line from where you live to where you are going

Interesting things I saw on the trip	

WHERE WE'RE STAYING

Draw a picture showing where you are staying during your vacation

Things I like about where we are staying

Interesting things I saw

I learned some interesting things about

My favourite meal was

I enjoyed playing with

I did not enjoy doing

GOING BACK HOME

I enjoyed my vacation because...

Did you make new friends?	
Would you want to go back there?	
Did you bring home any souvenirs?	

The thing that surprised me most was...

MY NEW FRIENDS

NAME	
EMAIL	
TELEPHONE NUMBER	

NAME	
EMAIL	
TELEPHONE NUMBER	

NAME	
EMAIL	
TELEPHONE NUMBER	

NAME	
EMAIL	
TELEPHONE NUMBER	

NAME	
EMAIL	
TELEPHONE NUMBER	

4

MY TRIP TO

WRITE, DRAW OR PASTE PHOTOGRAPHS ABOUT YOUR
ADVENTURES ON YOUR TRIP...

MY TRAVEL BUDDIES

NAME	
RELATIONSHIP TO YOU	
TELEPHONE NUMBER	

NAME	
RELATIONSHIP TO YOU	
TELEPHONE NUMBER	

NAME	
RELATIONSHIP TO YOU	
TELEPHONE NUMBER	

NAME	
RELATIONSHIP TO YOU	
TELEPHONE NUMBER	

NAME	
RELATIONSHIP TO YOU	
TELEPHONE NUMBER	

DON'T FORGET TO...

- Turn off your computer or ask your parents to do so
- Pack your travel guide books
- Take some travel stickers, pencils, a pack of colourful pens, glue sticks and adhesive tape for your travel journal.
- Take your favourite games to play on the trip and books to read

BEFORE THE TRIP

Where are you going?	
Is this your first visit?	
What do you know about the place?	Are you travelling by road, air, train or by sea?
How are you going to get there?	Does the country have a language different to yours?
Are you going to a different country?	
What do you think the place will be like?	
What are you looking forward to the most?	
What places would you visit during the trip?	For example theme parks, museums, zoo

LEAVING HOME

What is the weather like today?	
I travelled from...	to...
How far is the trip?	
How long will it take you to get there?	

Stick a map of where you are going.

Trace a line from where you live to where you are going

Interesting things I saw on the trip	

WHERE WE'RE STAYING

Draw a picture showing where you are staying during your vacation

Things I like about where we are staying	
Interesting things I saw	
I learned some interesting things about	
My favourite meal was	
I enjoyed playing with	
I did not enjoy doing	

GOING BACK HOME

I enjoyed my vacation because...

Did you make new friends?

Would you want to go back there?

Did you bring home any souvenirs?

The thing that surprised me most was...

MY NEW FRIENDS

NAME	
EMAIL	
TELEPHONE NUMBER	

NAME	
EMAIL	
TELEPHONE NUMBER	

NAME	
EMAIL	
TELEPHONE NUMBER	

NAME	
EMAIL	
TELEPHONE NUMBER	

NAME	
EMAIL	
TELEPHONE NUMBER	

5

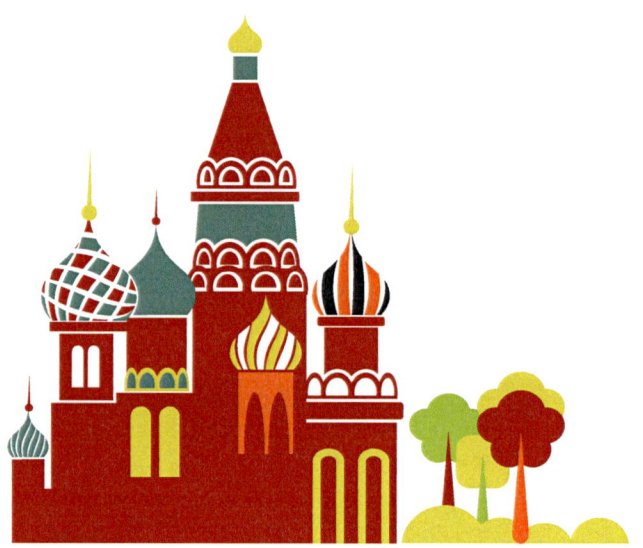

MY TRIP TO

WRITE, DRAW OR PASTE PHOTOGRAPHS ABOUT YOUR
ADVENTURES ON YOUR TRIP...

MY TRAVEL BUDDIES

NAME	
RELATIONSHIP TO YOU	
TELEPHONE NUMBER	

NAME	
RELATIONSHIP TO YOU	
TELEPHONE NUMBER	

NAME	
RELATIONSHIP TO YOU	
TELEPHONE NUMBER	

NAME	
RELATIONSHIP TO YOU	
TELEPHONE NUMBER	

NAME	
RELATIONSHIP TO YOU	
TELEPHONE NUMBER	

DON'T FORGET TO...

- Turn off your computer or ask your parents to do so
- Pack your travel guide books
- Take some travel stickers, pencils, a pack of colourful pens, glue sticks and adhesive tape for your travel journal.
- Take your favourite games to play on the trip and books to read

BEFORE THE TRIP

Where are you going?	
Is this your first visit?	
What do you know about the place?	Are you travelling by road, air, train or by sea?
How are you going to get there?	Does the country have a language different to yours?
Are you going to a different country?	
What do you think the place will be like?	
What are you looking forward to the most?	
What places would you visit during the trip?	For example theme parks, museums, zoo

LEAVING HOME

What is the weather like today?	
I travelled from...	to...
How far is the trip?	
How long will it take you to get there?	

Stick a map of where you are going.

Trace a line from where you live to where you are going

Interesting things I saw on the trip	

WHERE WE'RE STAYING

Draw a picture showing where you are staying during your vacation

Things I like about where we are staying	
Interesting things I saw	
I learned some interesting things about	
My favourite meal was	
I enjoyed playing with	
I did not enjoy doing	

GOING BACK HOME

I enjoyed my vacation because...

Did you make new friends?

Would you want to go back there?

Did you bring home any souvenirs?

The thing that surprised me most was...

MY NEW FRIENDS

NAME	
EMAIL	
TELEPHONE NUMBER	

NAME	
EMAIL	
TELEPHONE NUMBER	

NAME	
EMAIL	
TELEPHONE NUMBER	

NAME	
EMAIL	
TELEPHONE NUMBER	

NAME	
EMAIL	
TELEPHONE NUMBER	

NOTES